I0476631

Wisdom

Adult Coloring Book

by Asma Zergui

http://www.asmazergui.com

ISBN-13:
978-1515074236

ISBN-10:
1515074234

DEDICATION

To my parents, thank you for all that you've done for me.

Peace comes from within. Do not seek it without.

Buddha

Either I will find a way, or I will make one.

Philip Sidney

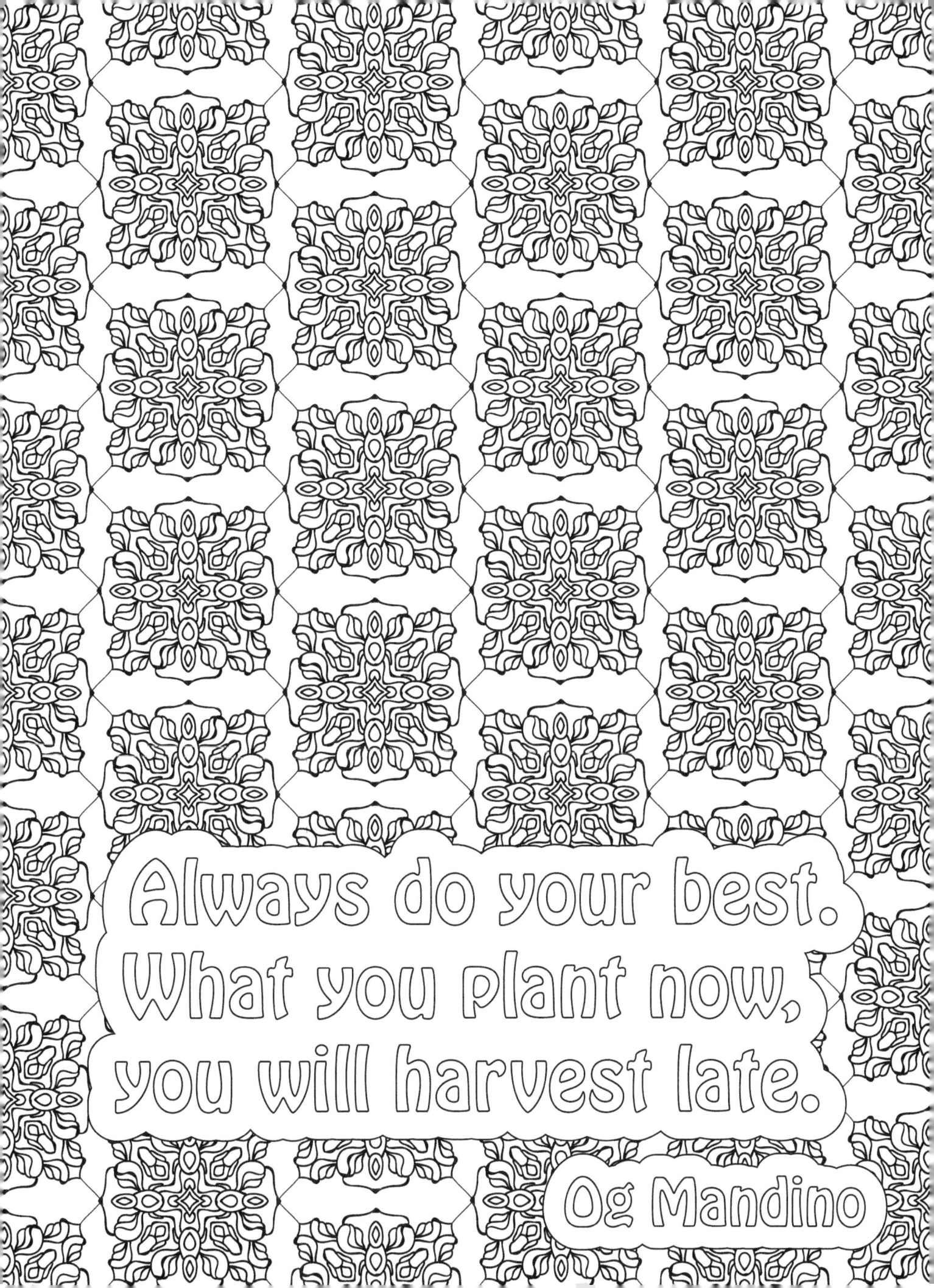

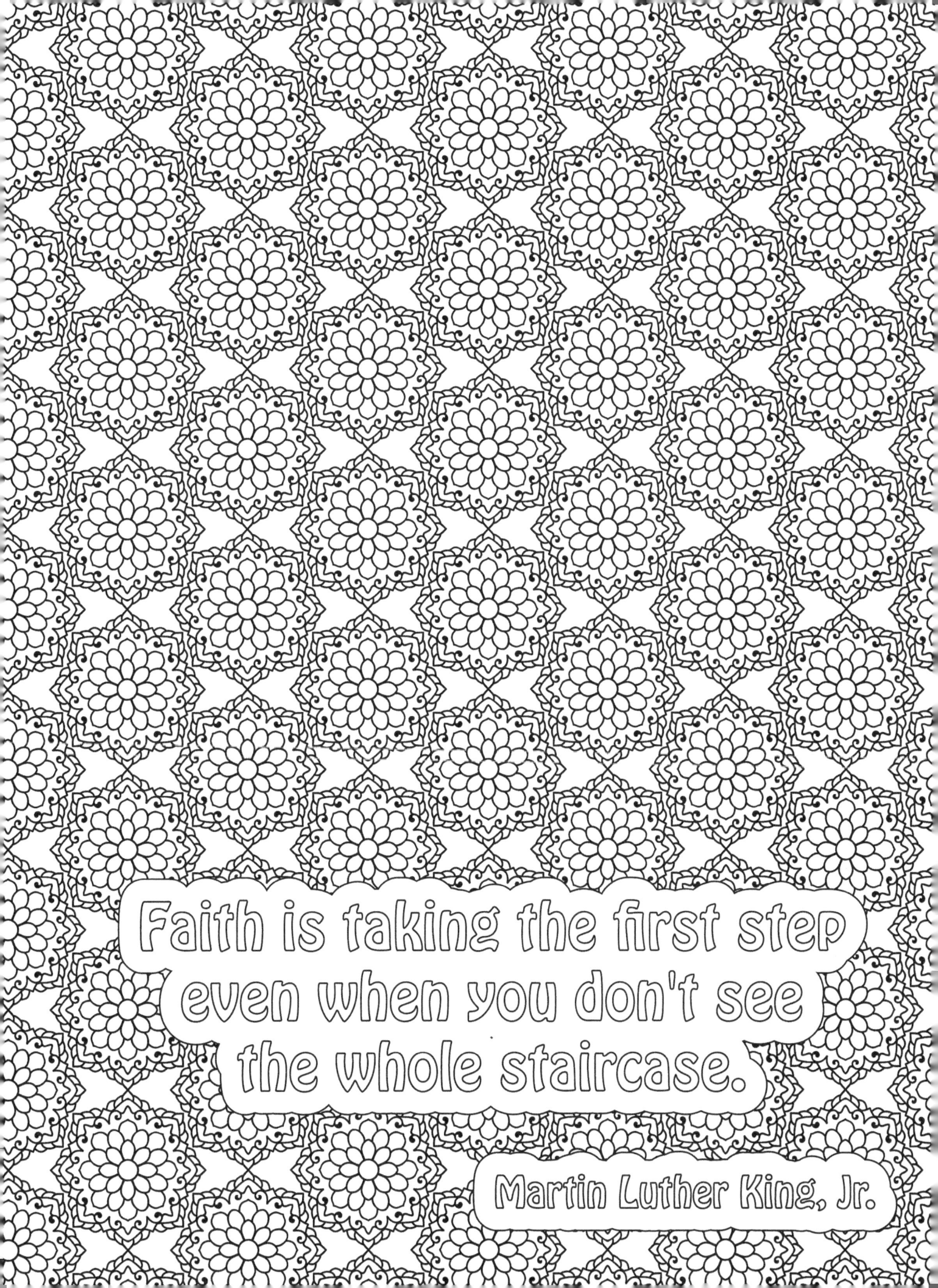

Faith is taking the first step even when you don't see the whole staircase.

Martin Luther King, Jr.

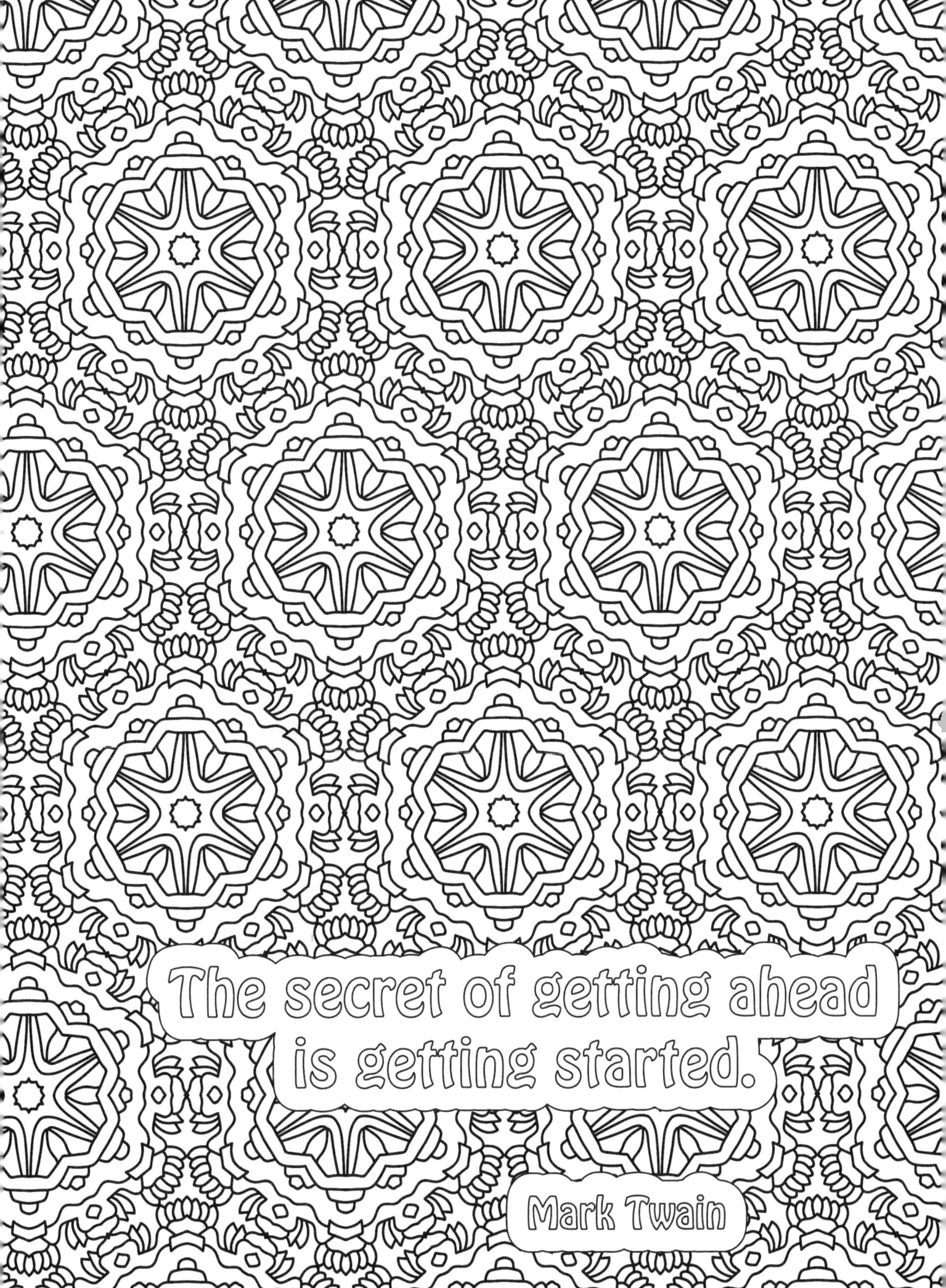

The secret of getting ahead is getting started.

Mark Twain

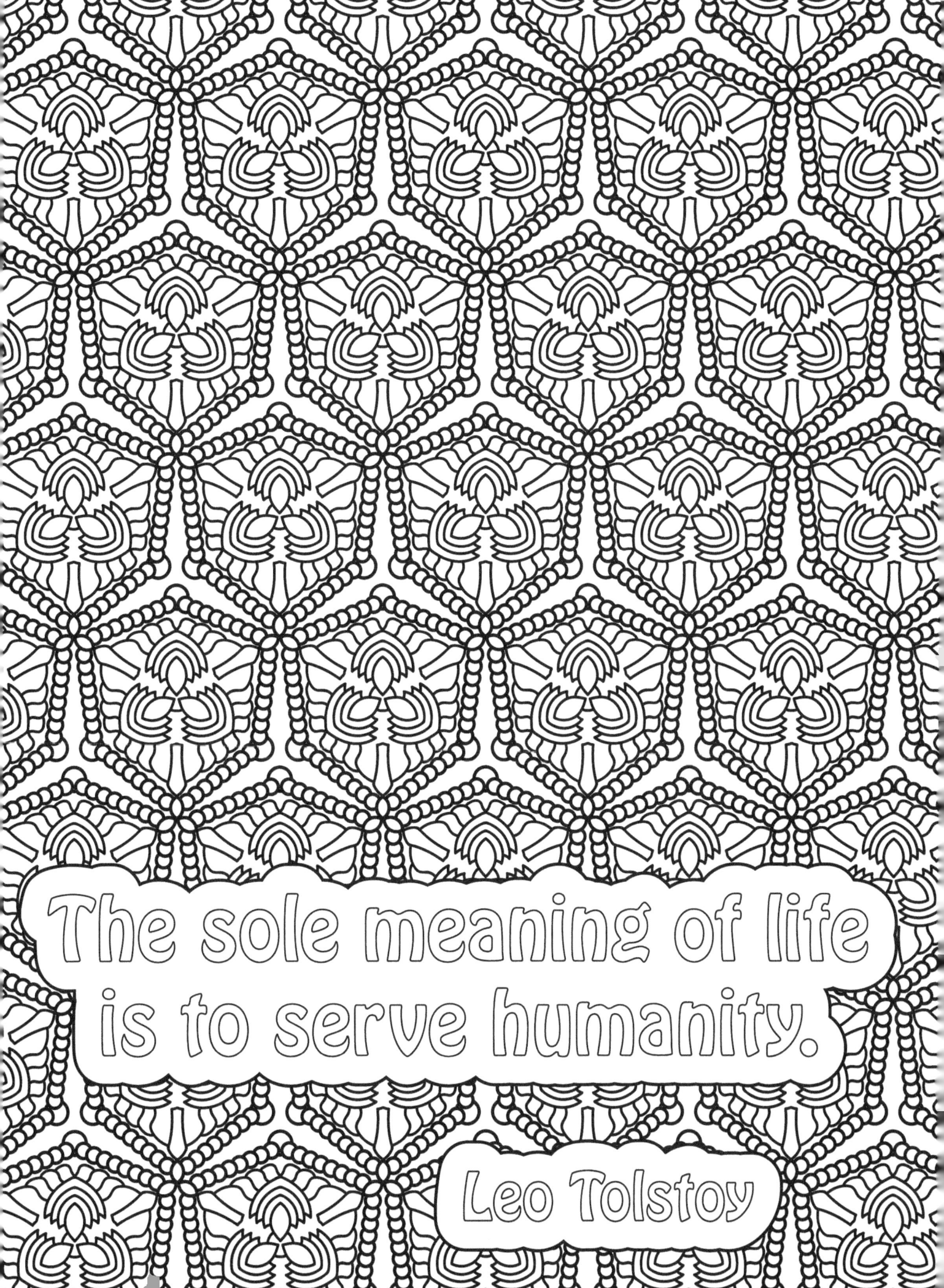

The sole meaning of life is to serve humanity.

Leo Tolstoy

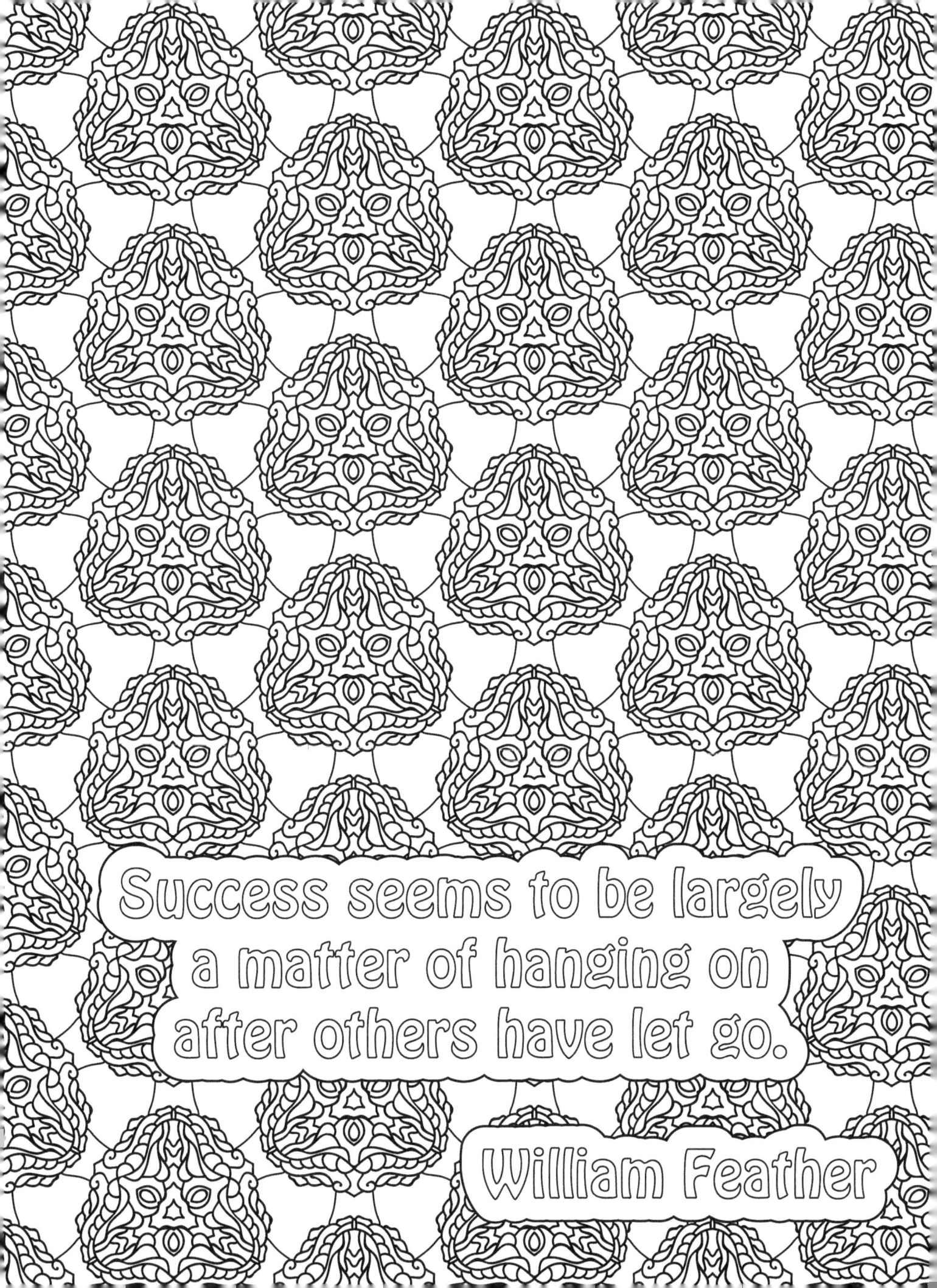

Success seems to be largely
a matter of hanging on
after others have let go.

William Feather

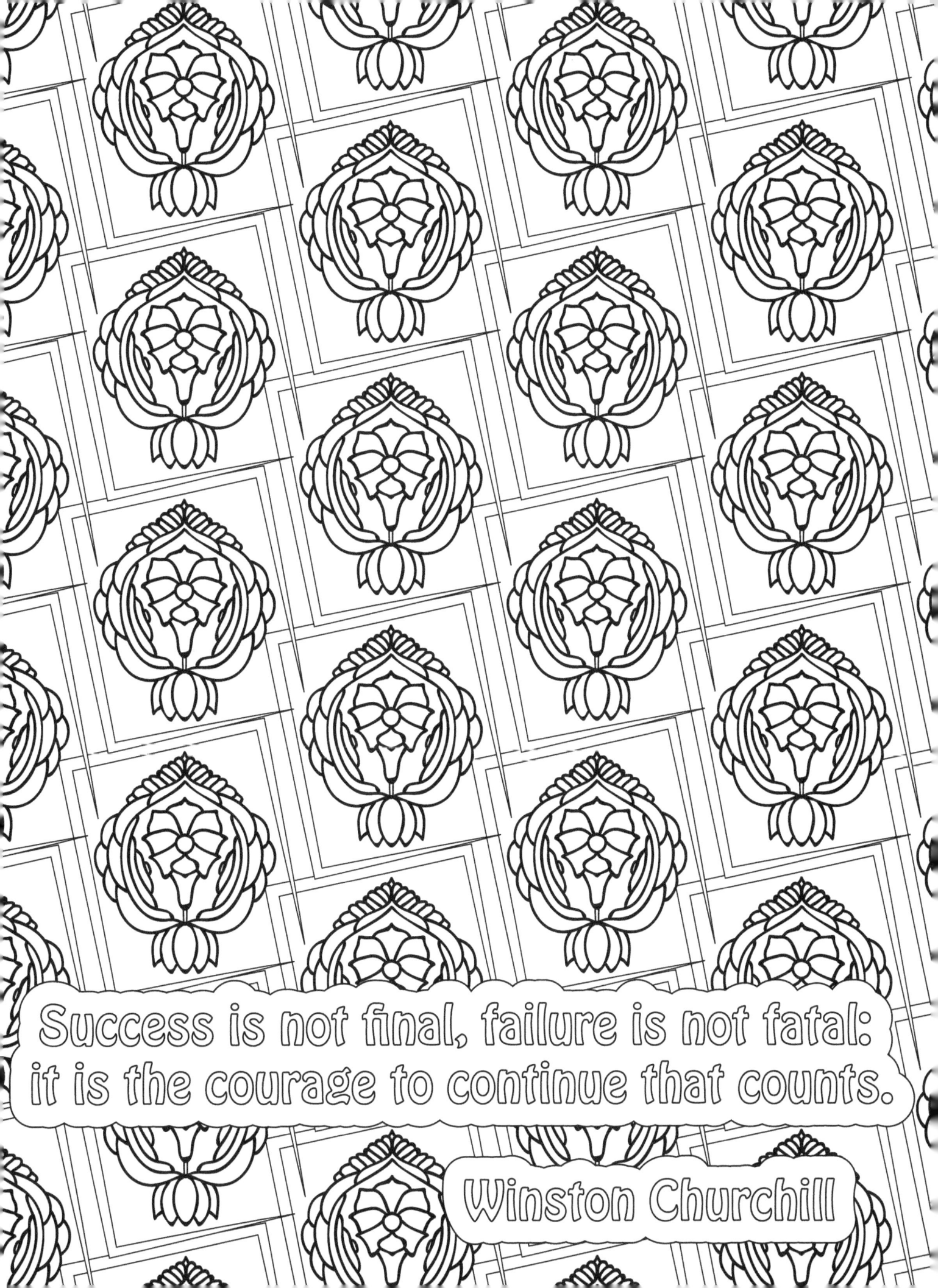

Success is not final, failure is not fatal: it is the courage to continue that counts.

Winston Churchill

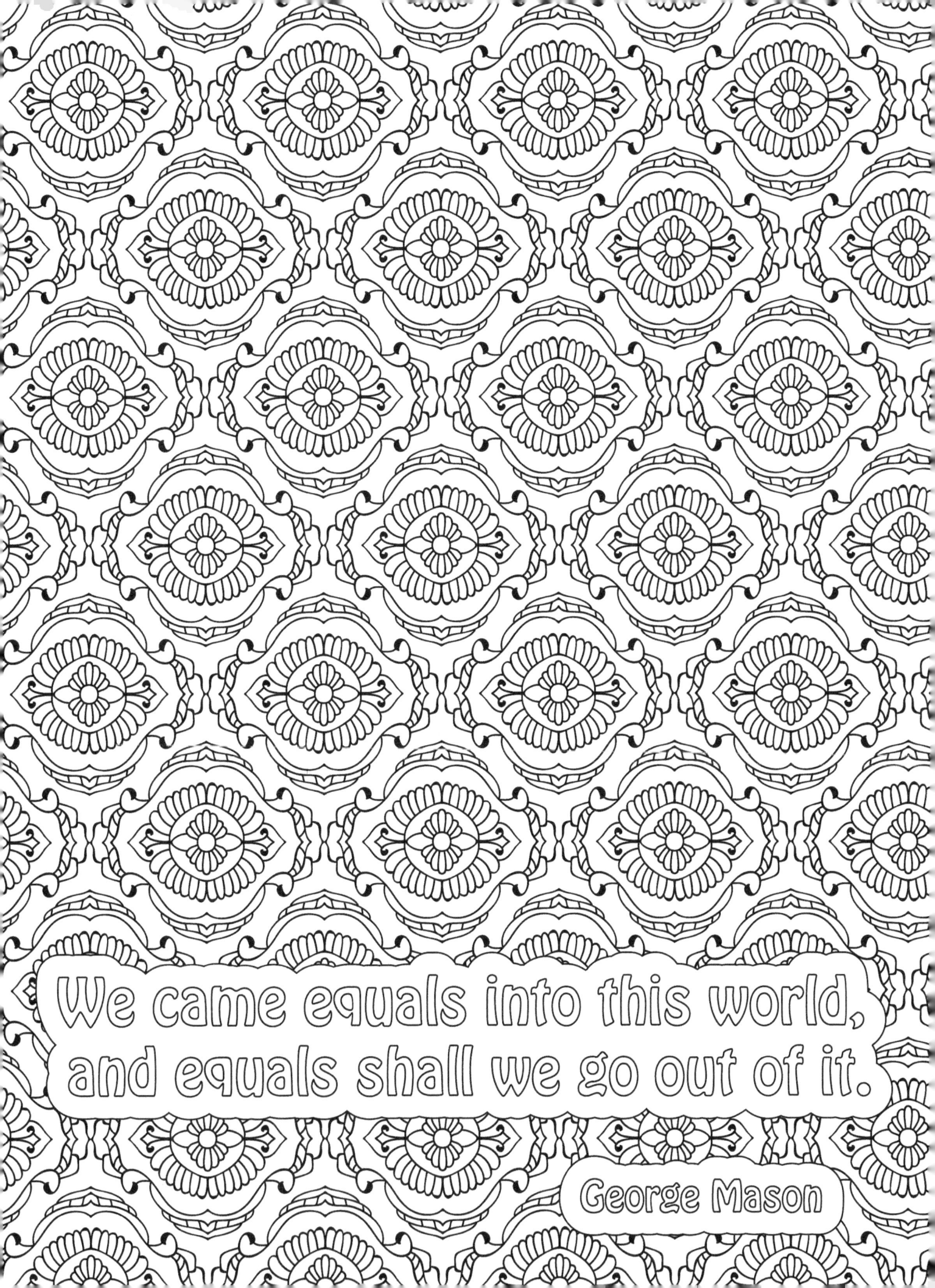

We came equals into this world, and equals shall we go out of it.

George Mason

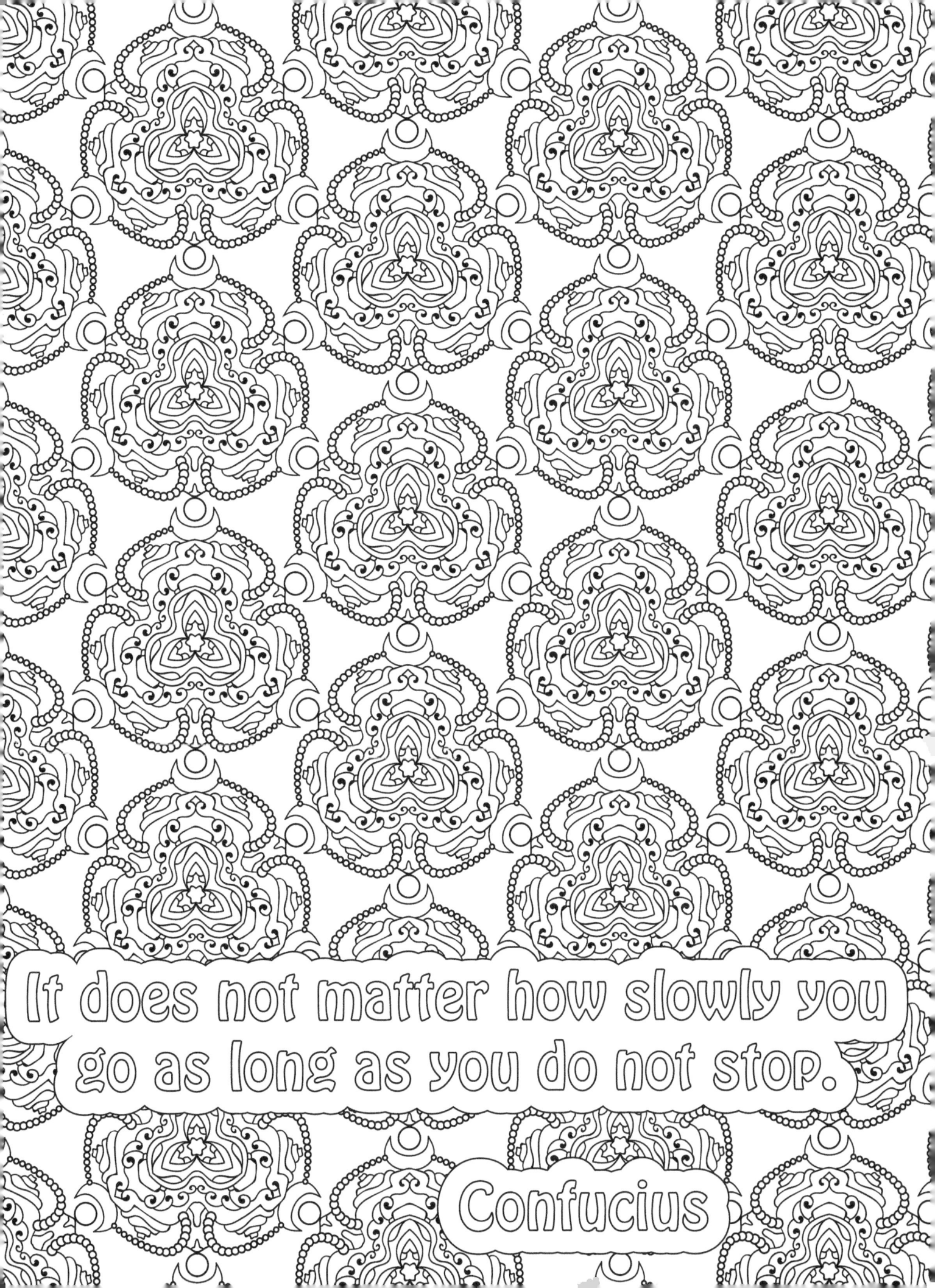

It does not matter how slowly you go as long as you do not stop.

Confucius

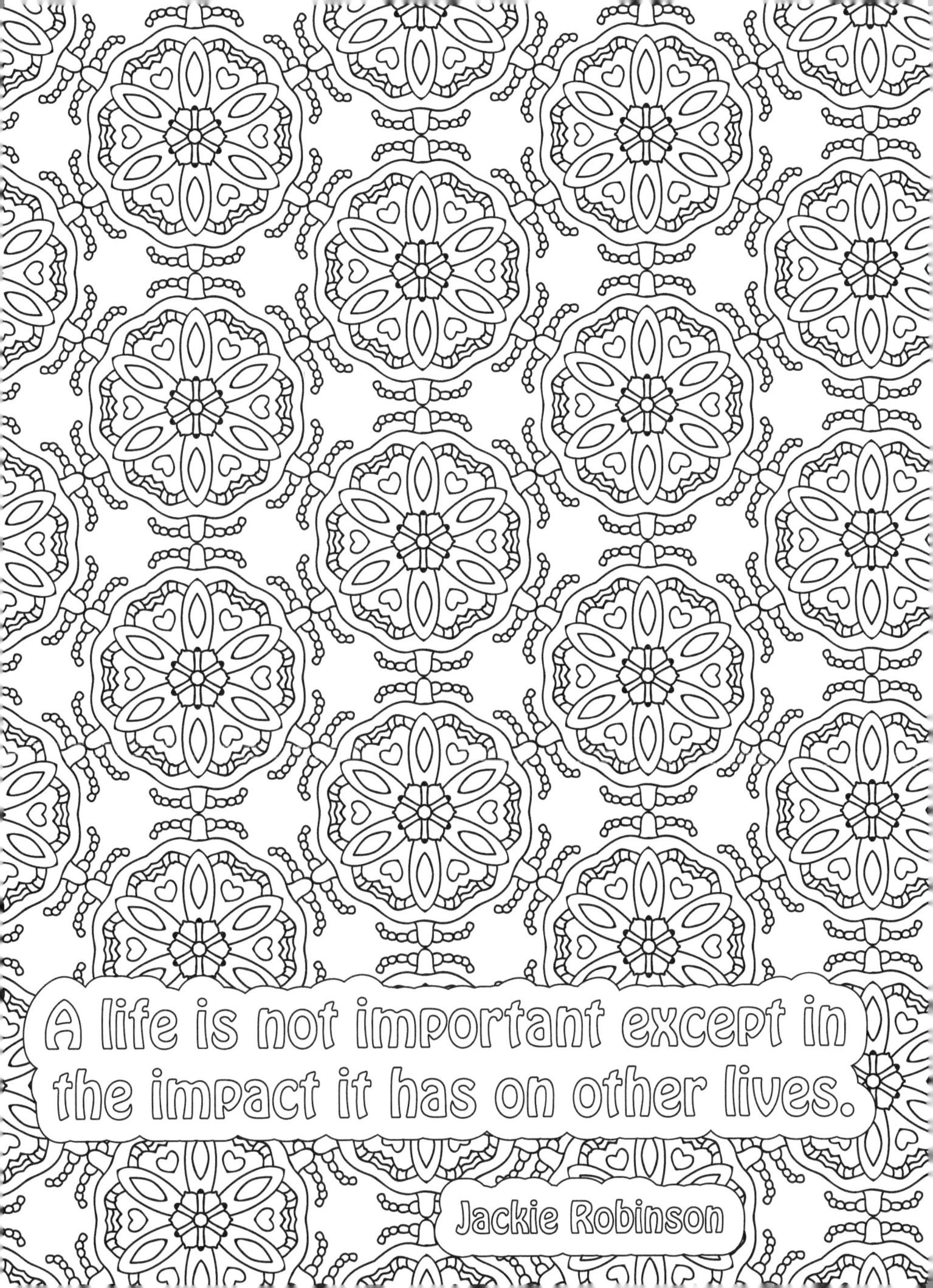

A life is not important except in the impact it has on other lives.

Jackie Robinson

Blessed are those who give
without remembering
and take without forgetting.

Elizabeth Bibesco

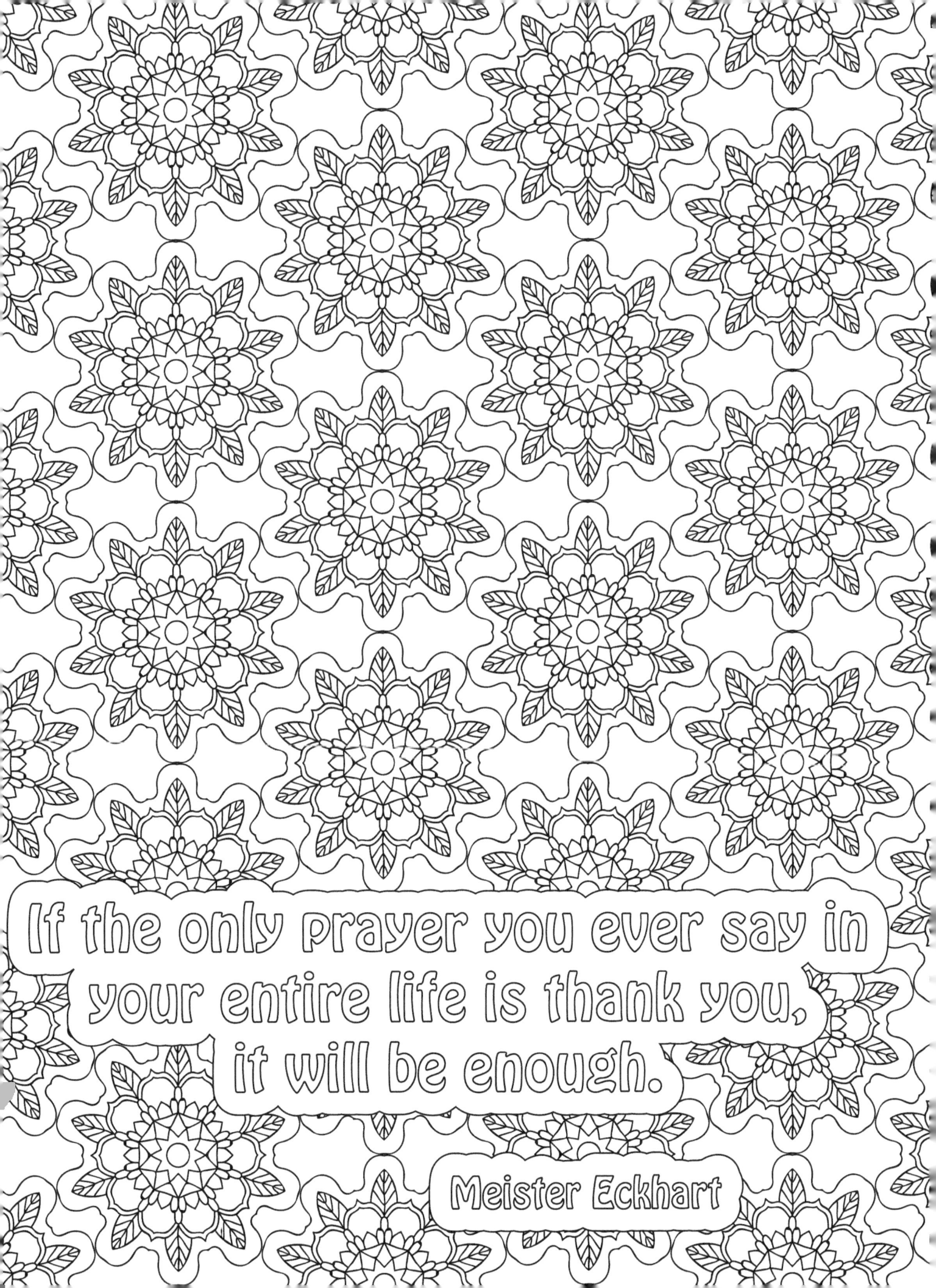

If the only prayer you ever say in your entire life is thank you, it will be enough.

Meister Eckhart

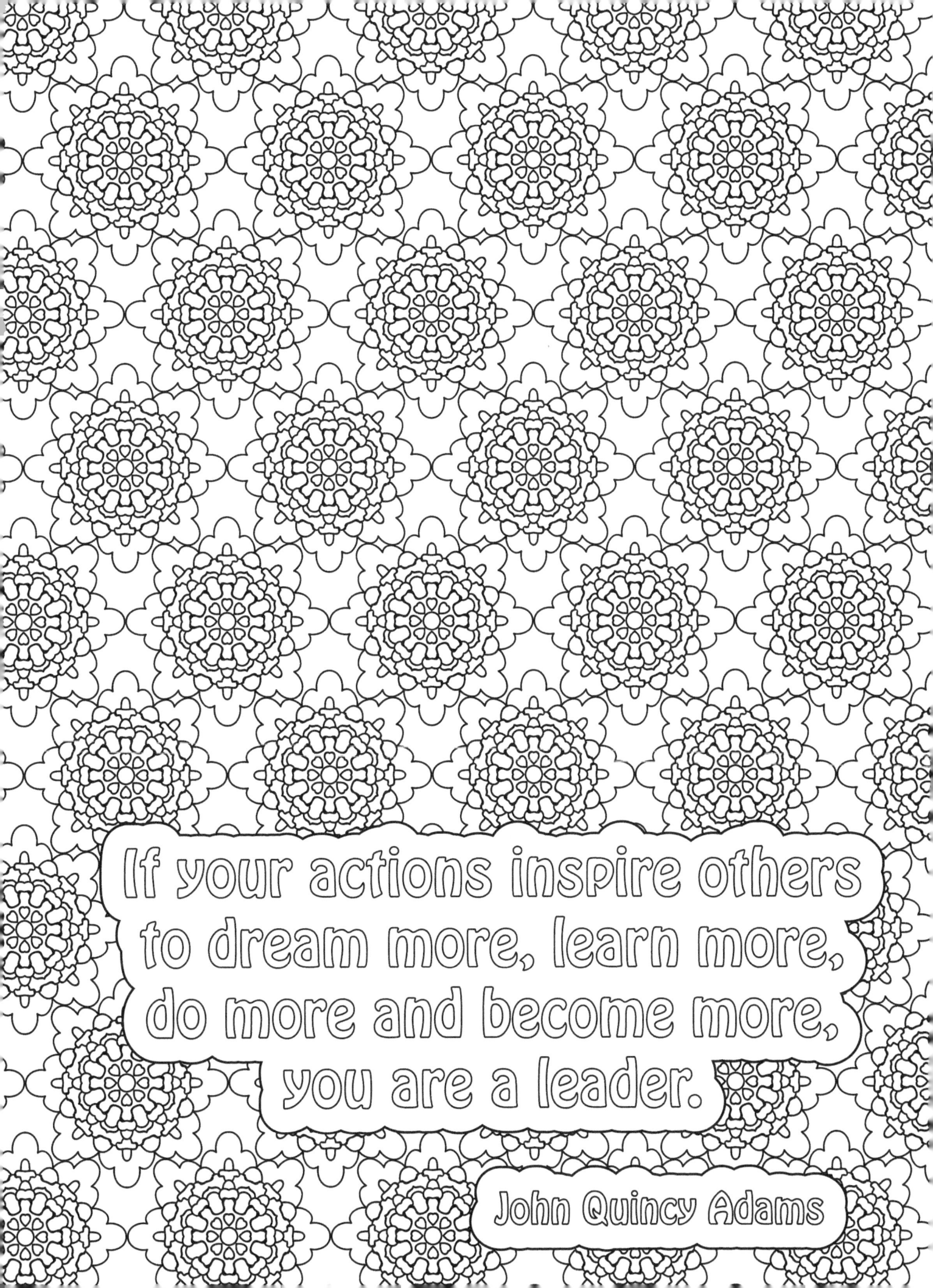

If your actions inspire others to dream more, learn more, do more and become more, you are a leader.

John Quincy Adams

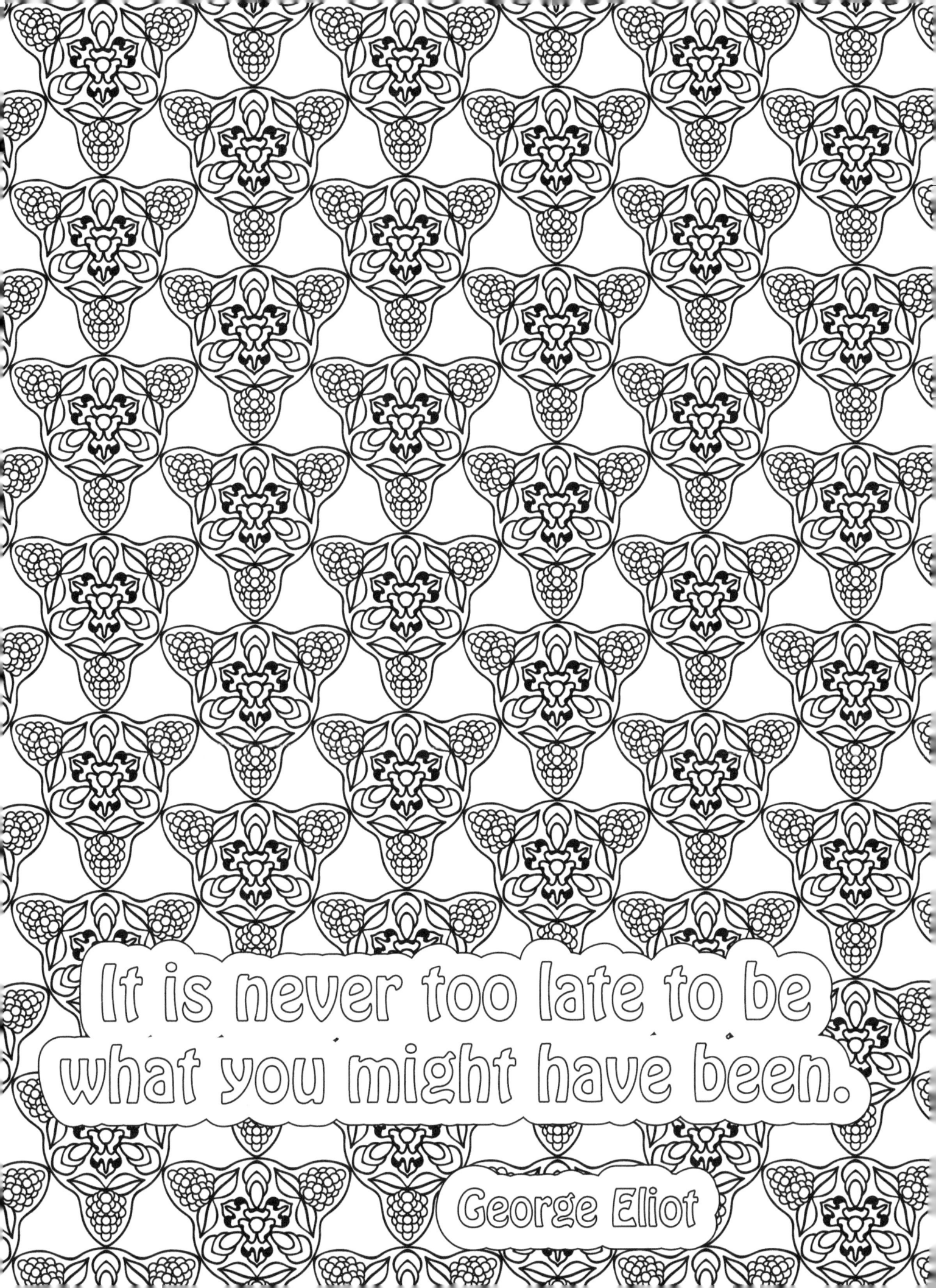

It is never too late to be what you might have been.

George Eliot

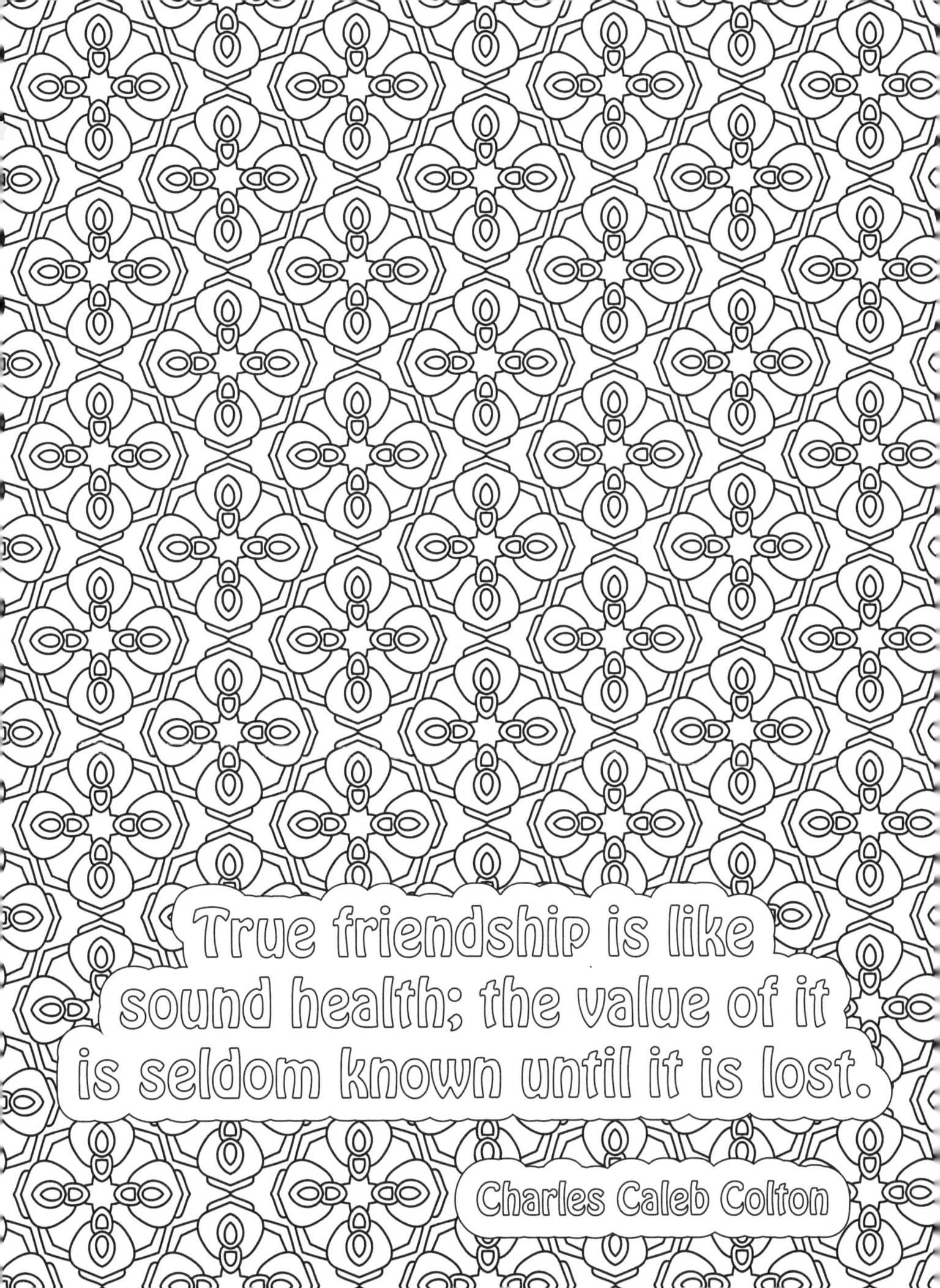

True friendship is like sound health; the value of it is seldom known until it is lost.

Charles Caleb Colton

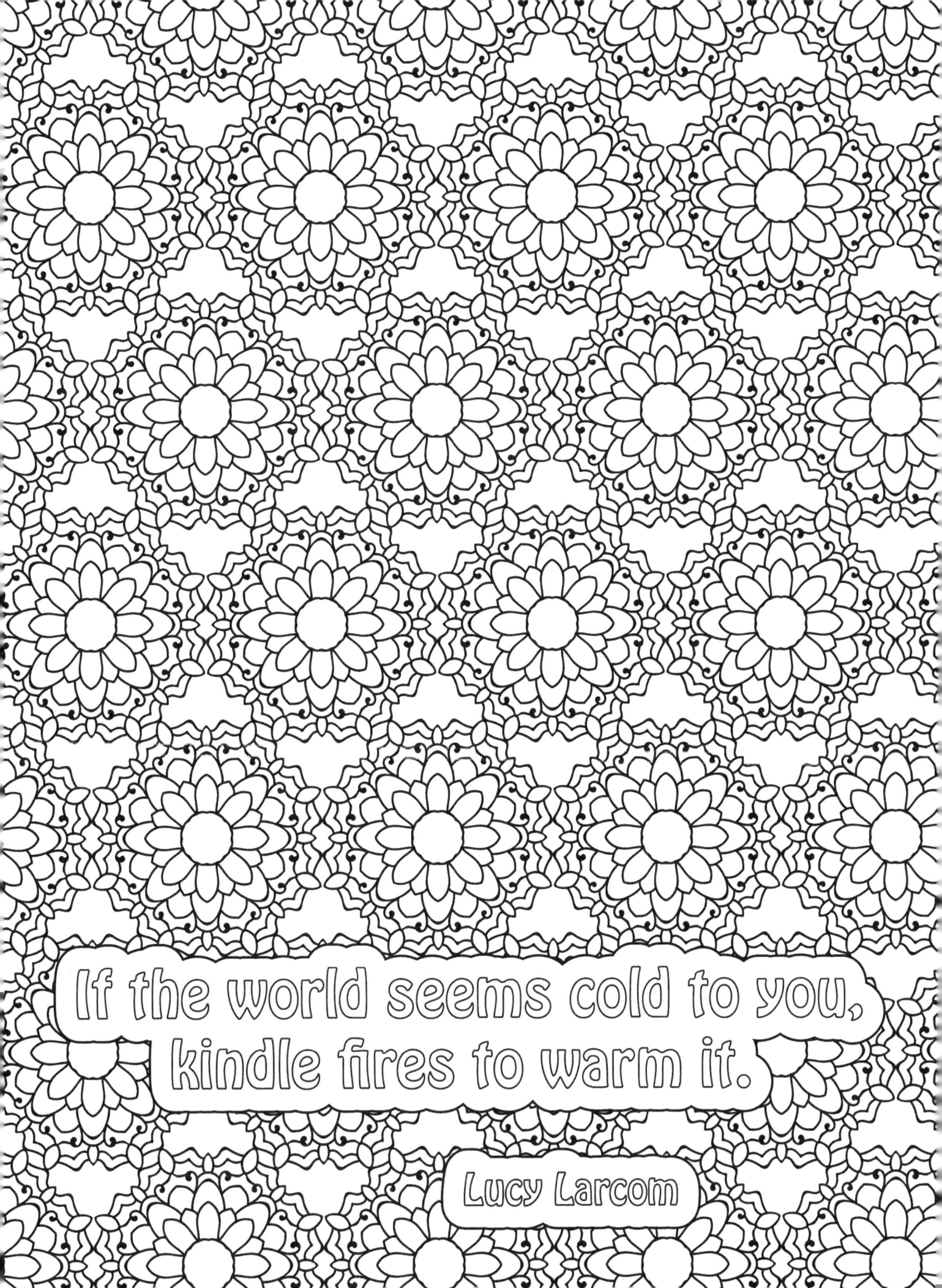

If the world seems cold to you,
kindle fires to warm it.

Lucy Larcom

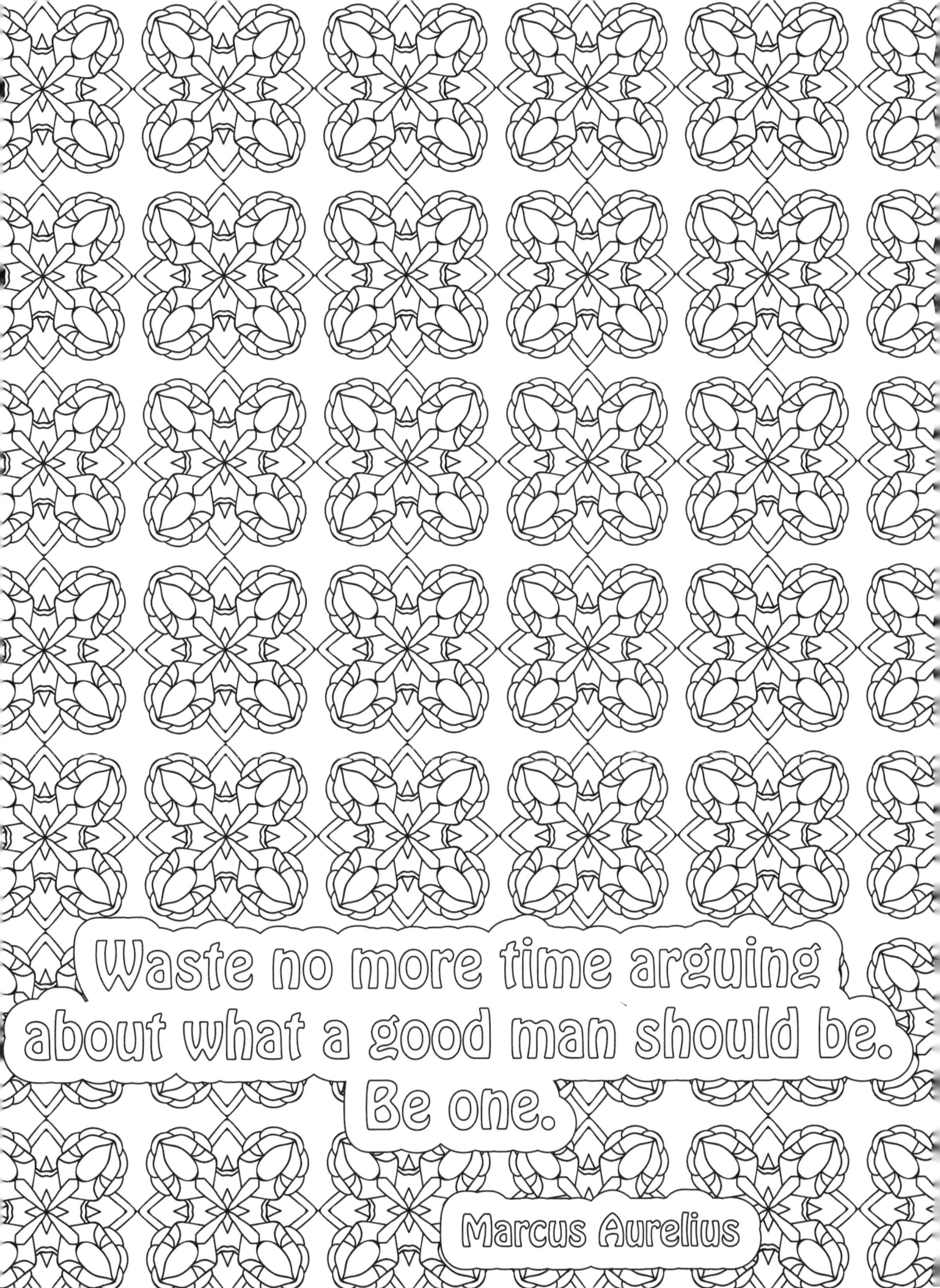

Waste no more time arguing about what a good man should be. Be one.

Marcus Aurelius

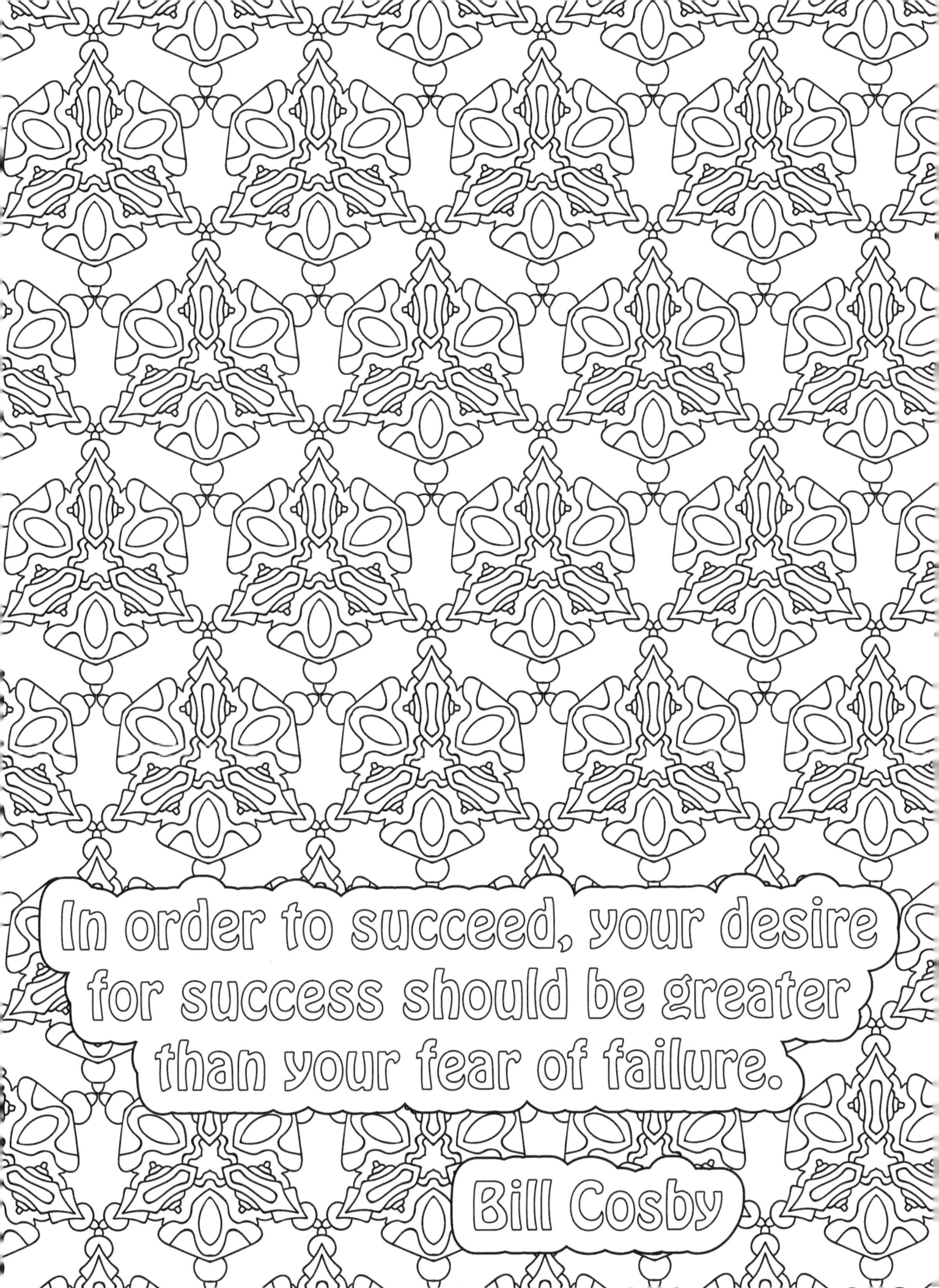

In order to succeed, your desire for success should be greater than your fear of failure.

Bill Cosby

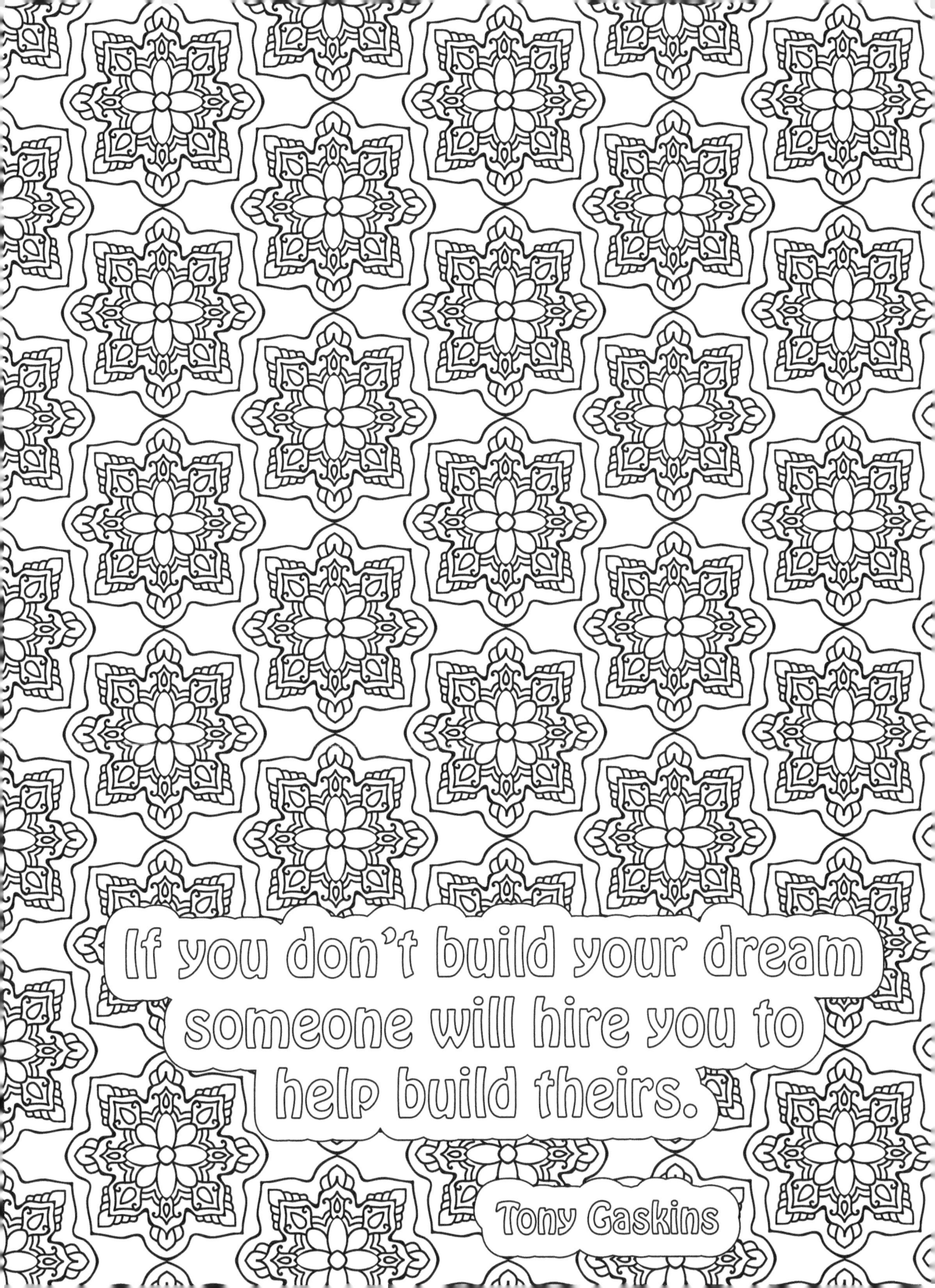

If you don't build your dream someone will hire you to help build theirs.

Tony Gaskins

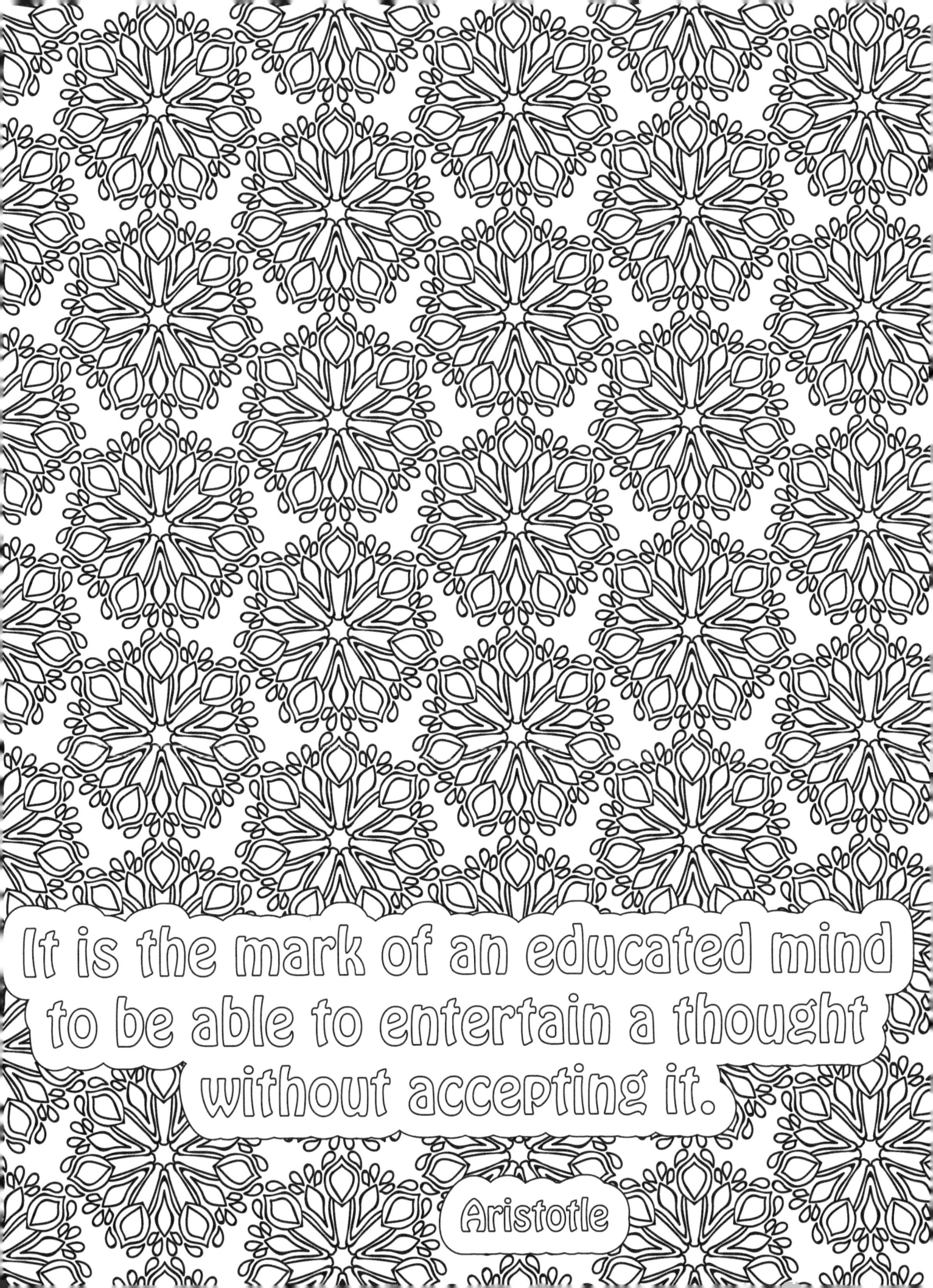

It is the mark of an educated mind to be able to entertain a thought without accepting it.

Aristotle

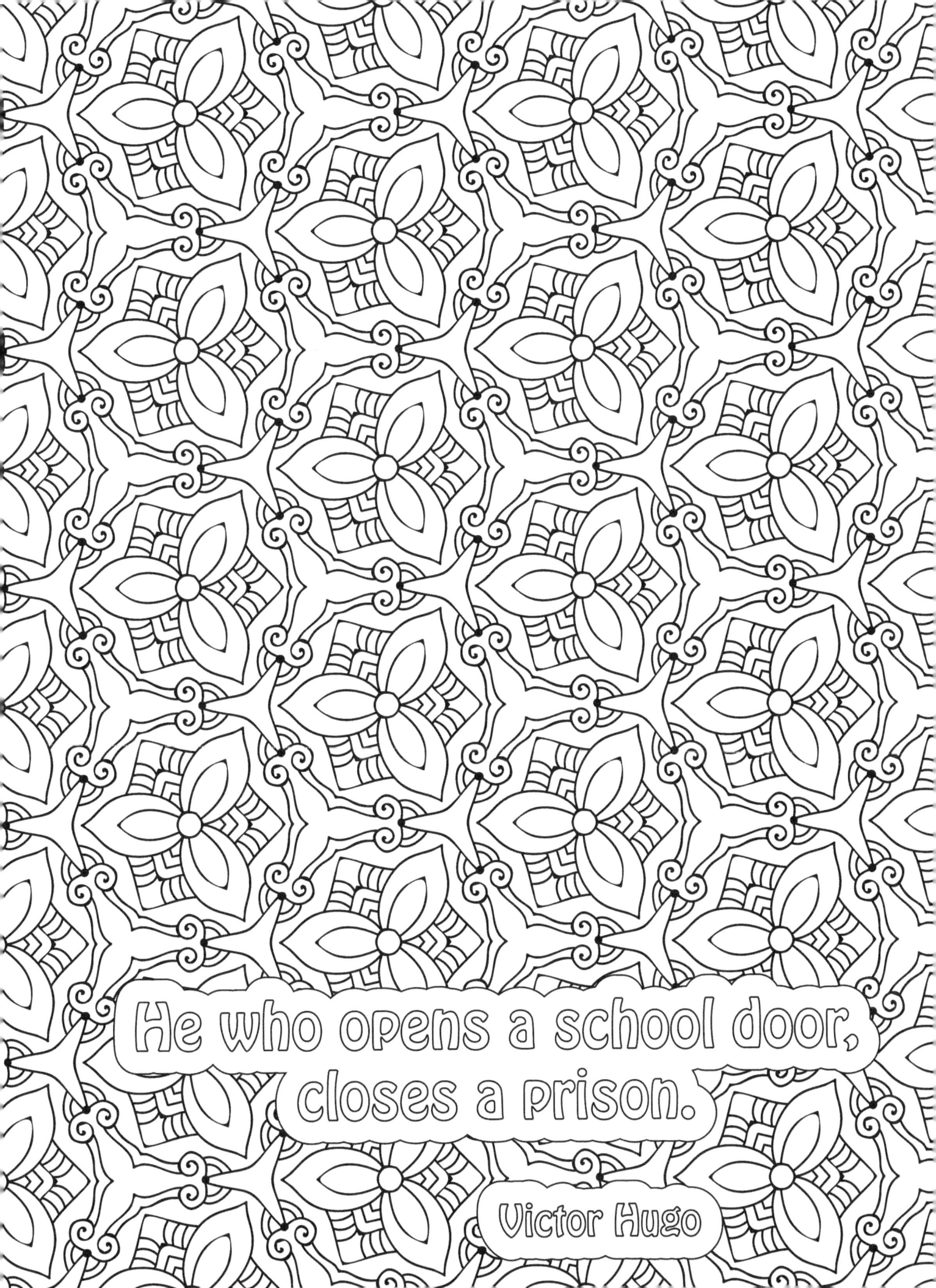

He who opens a school door, closes a prison.

Victor Hugo

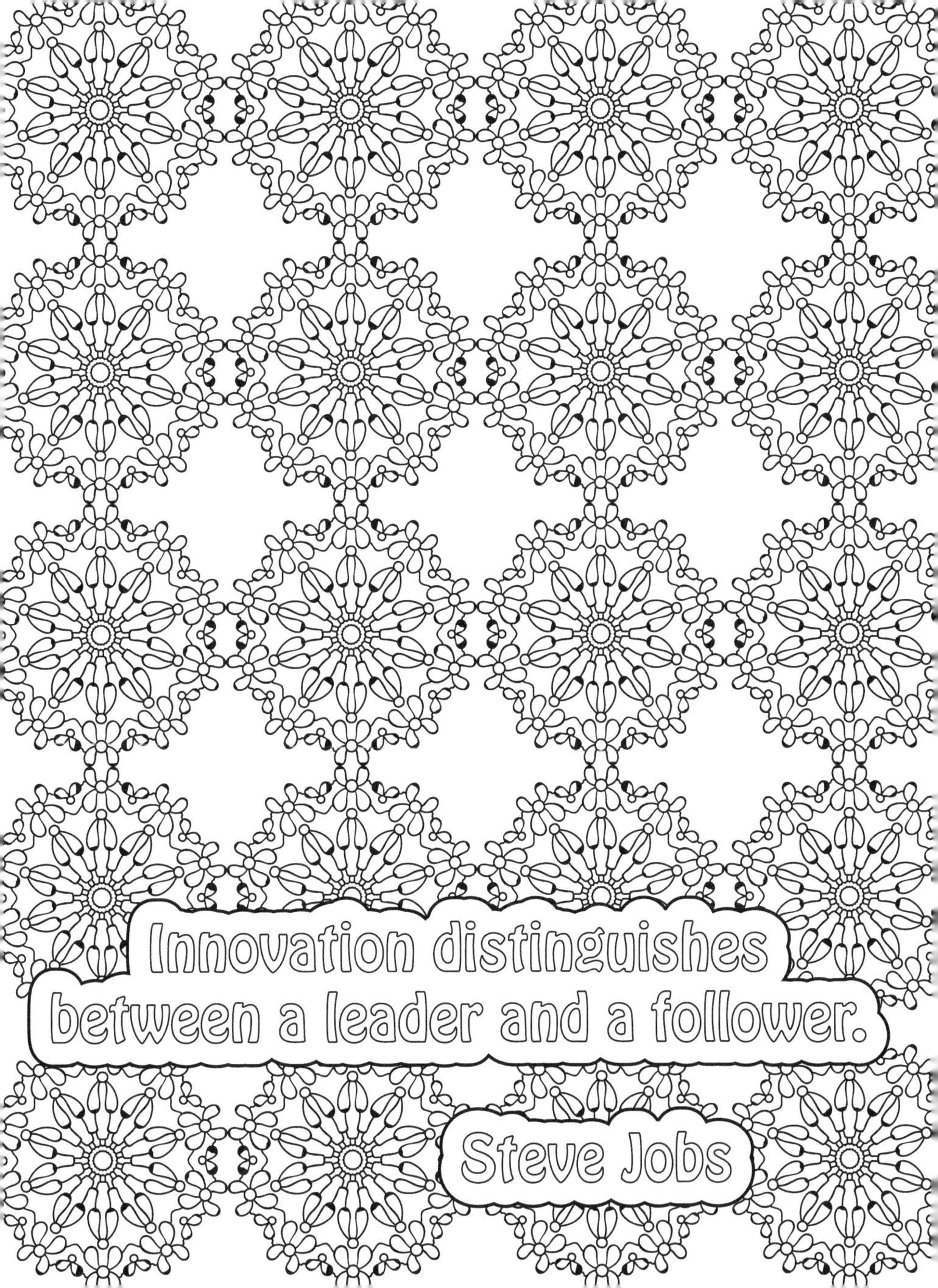

Innovation distinguishes between a leader and a follower.

Steve Jobs

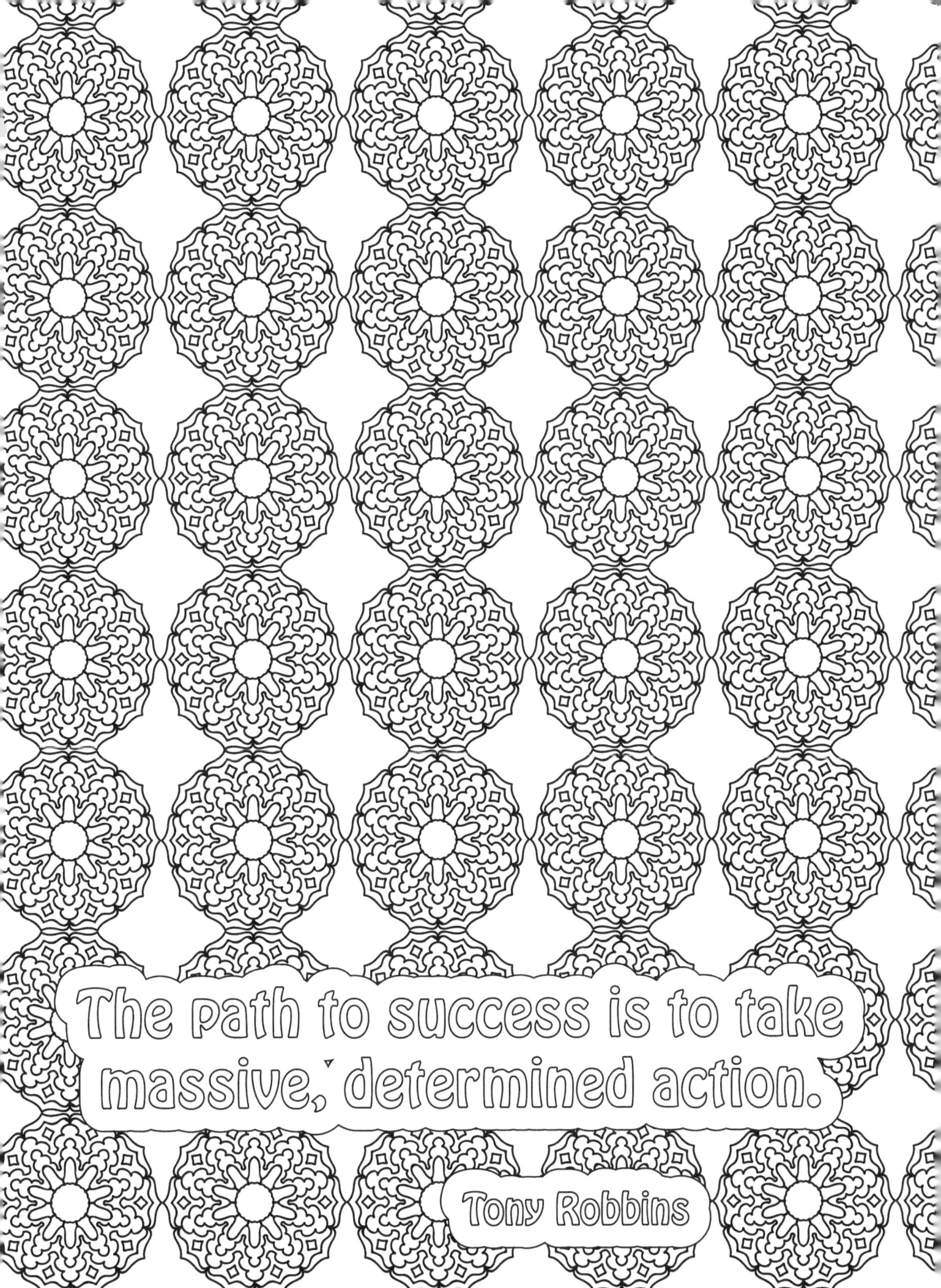

The path to success is to take massive, determined action.

Tony Robbins

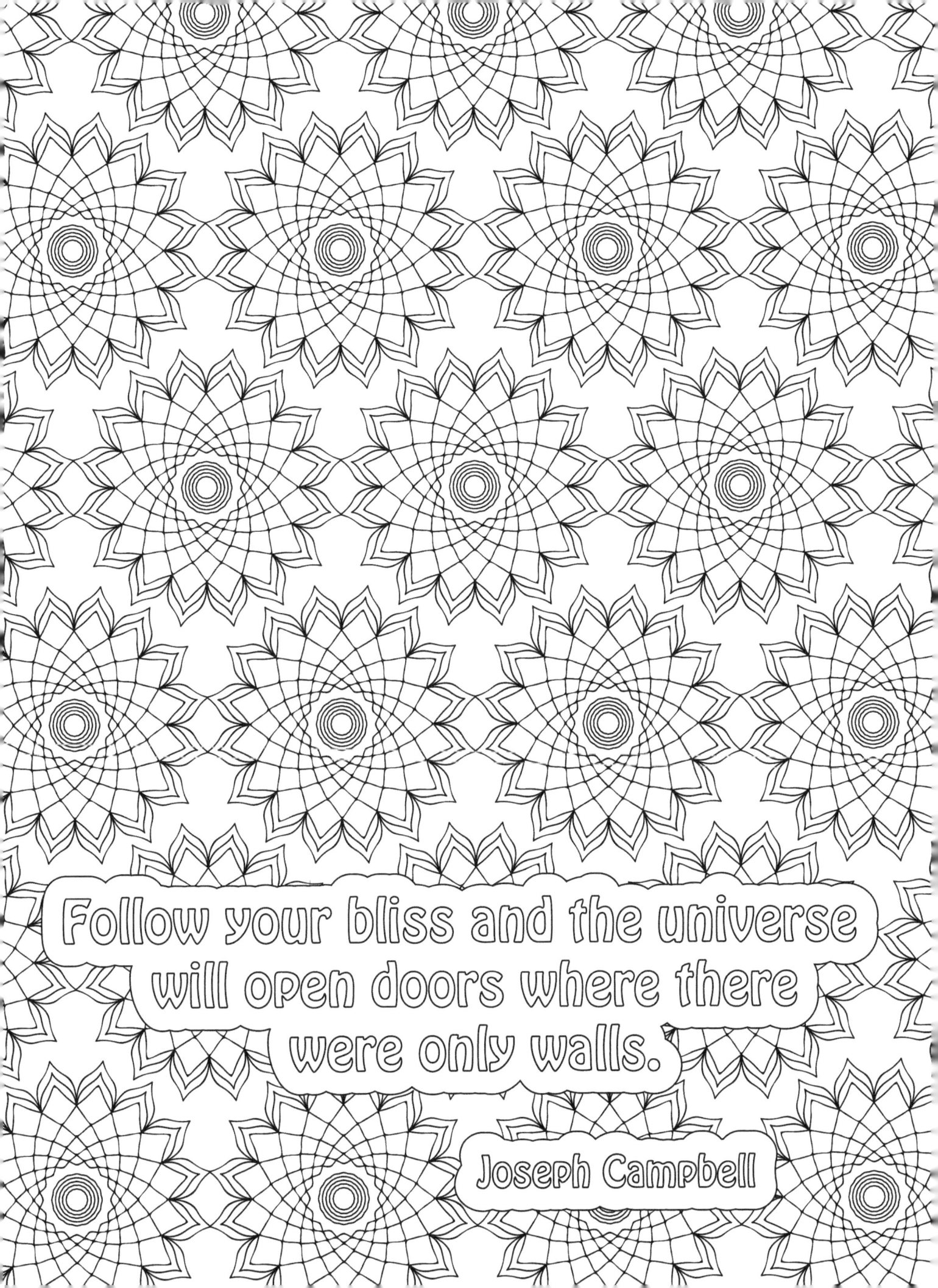

Follow your bliss and the universe
will open doors where there
were only walls.

Joseph Campbell

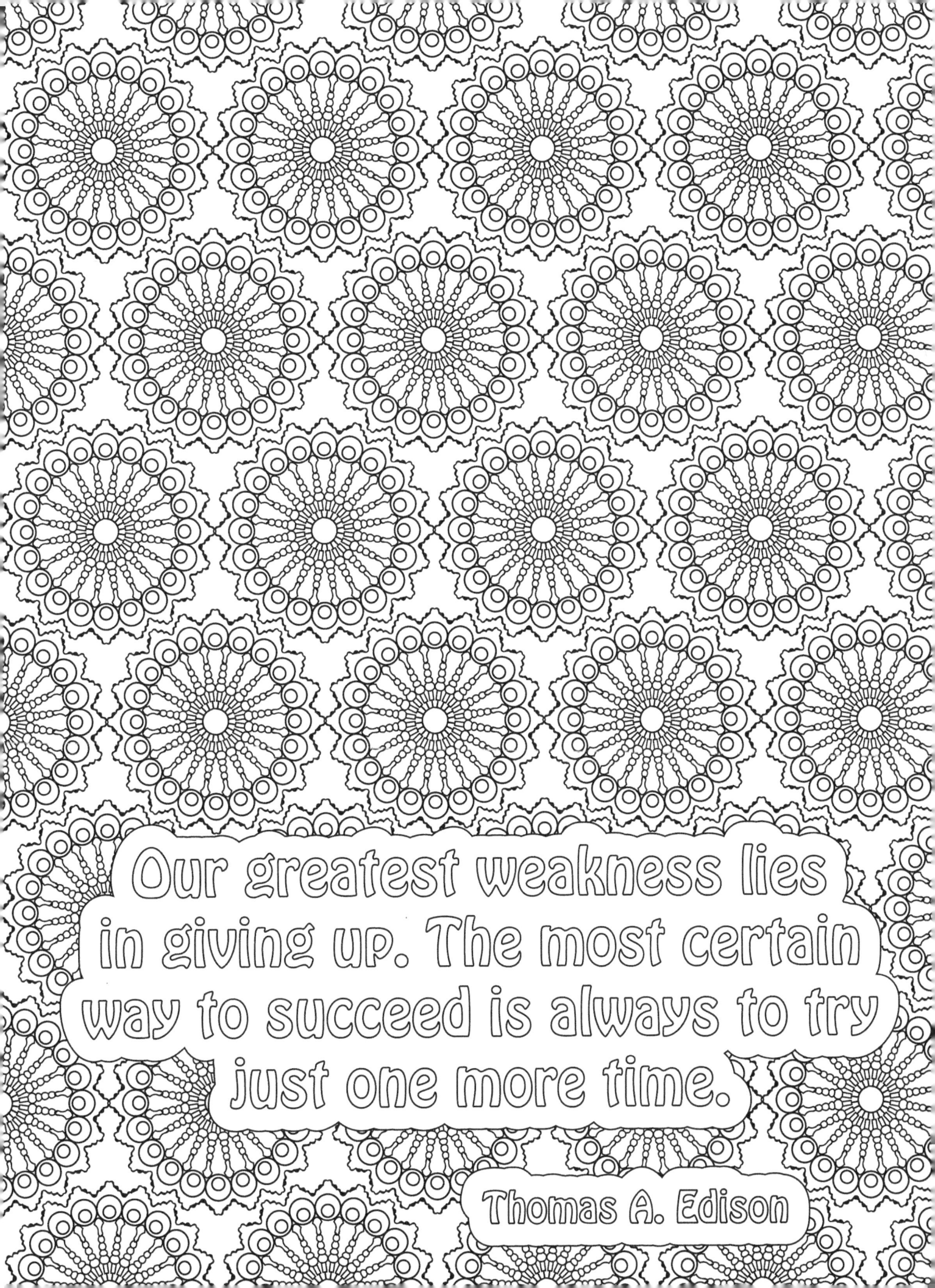

Our greatest weakness lies in giving up. The most certain way to succeed is always to try just one more time.

Thomas A. Edison

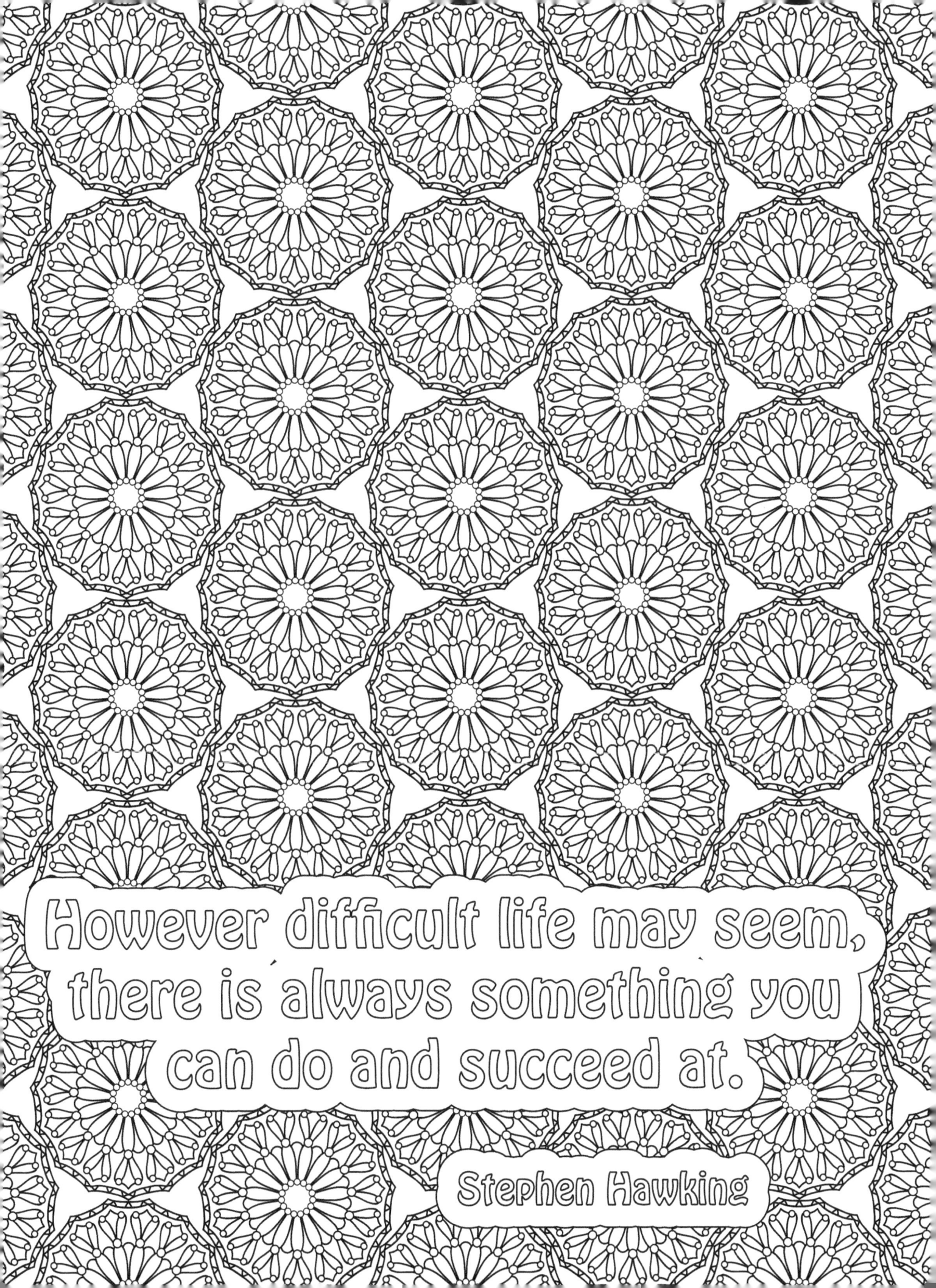

However difficult life may seem, there is always something you can do and succeed at.

Stephen Hawking

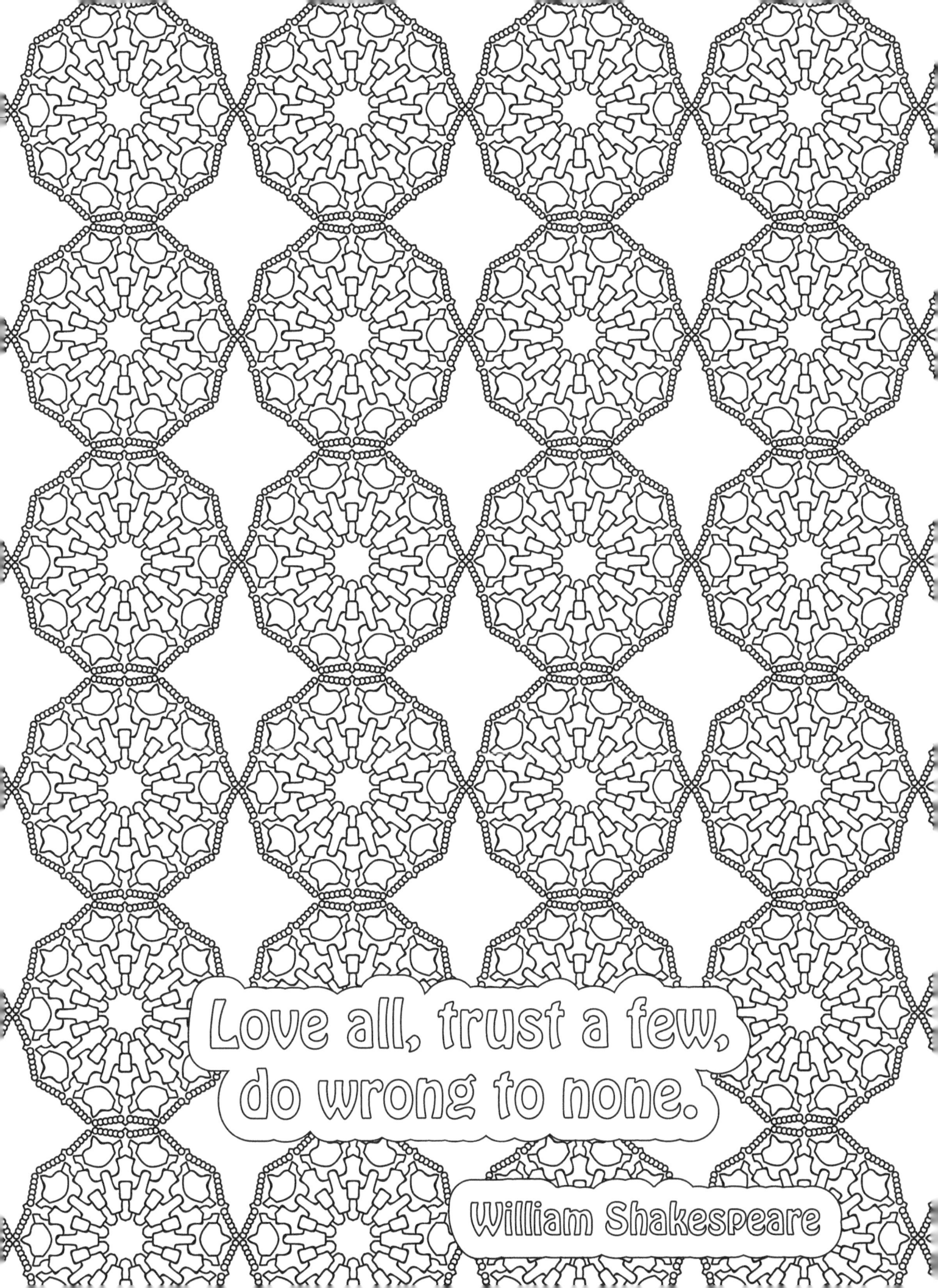

Love all, trust a few,
do wrong to none.

William Shakespeare

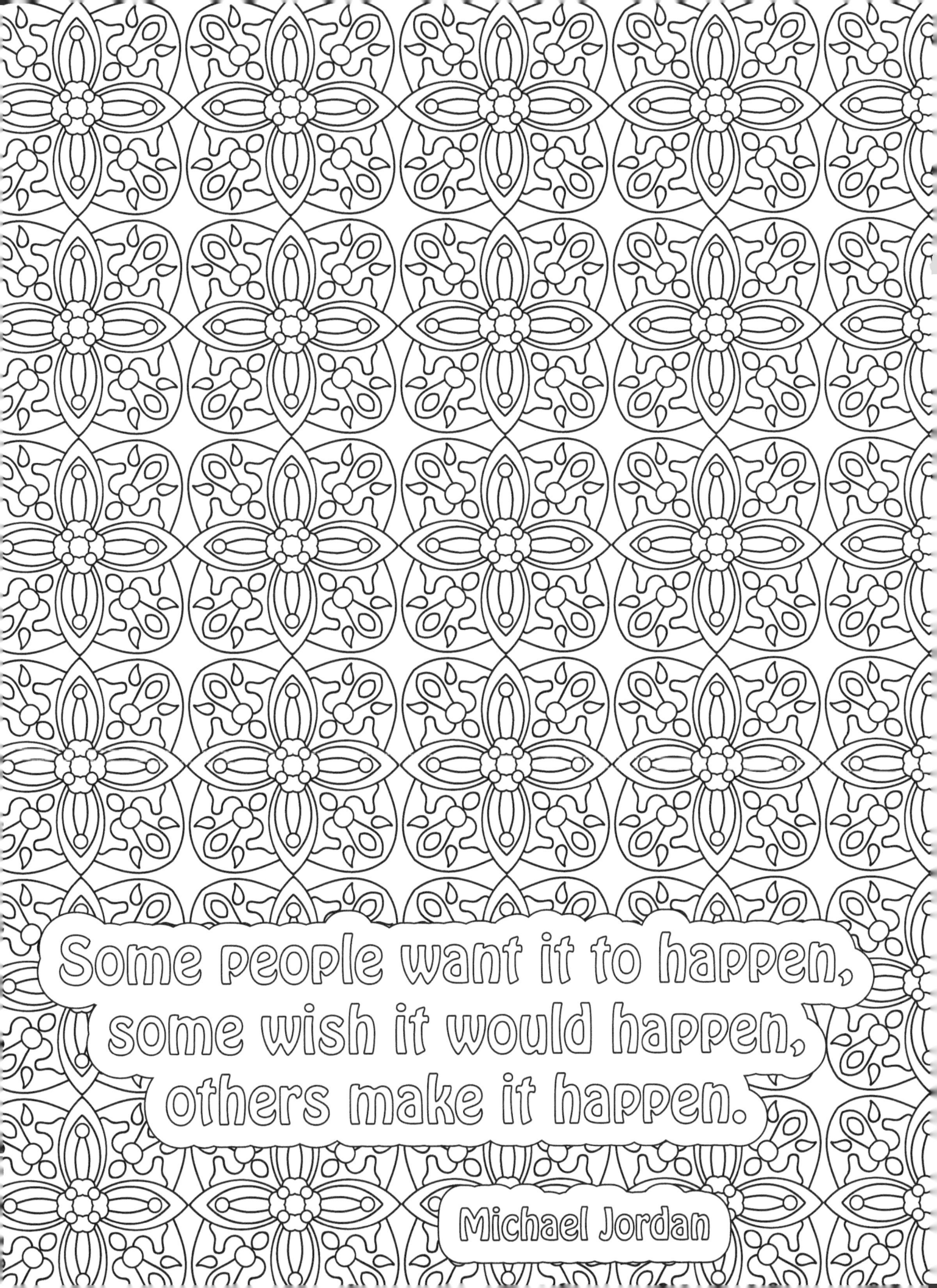

Some people want it to happen, some wish it would happen, others make it happen.

Michael Jordan

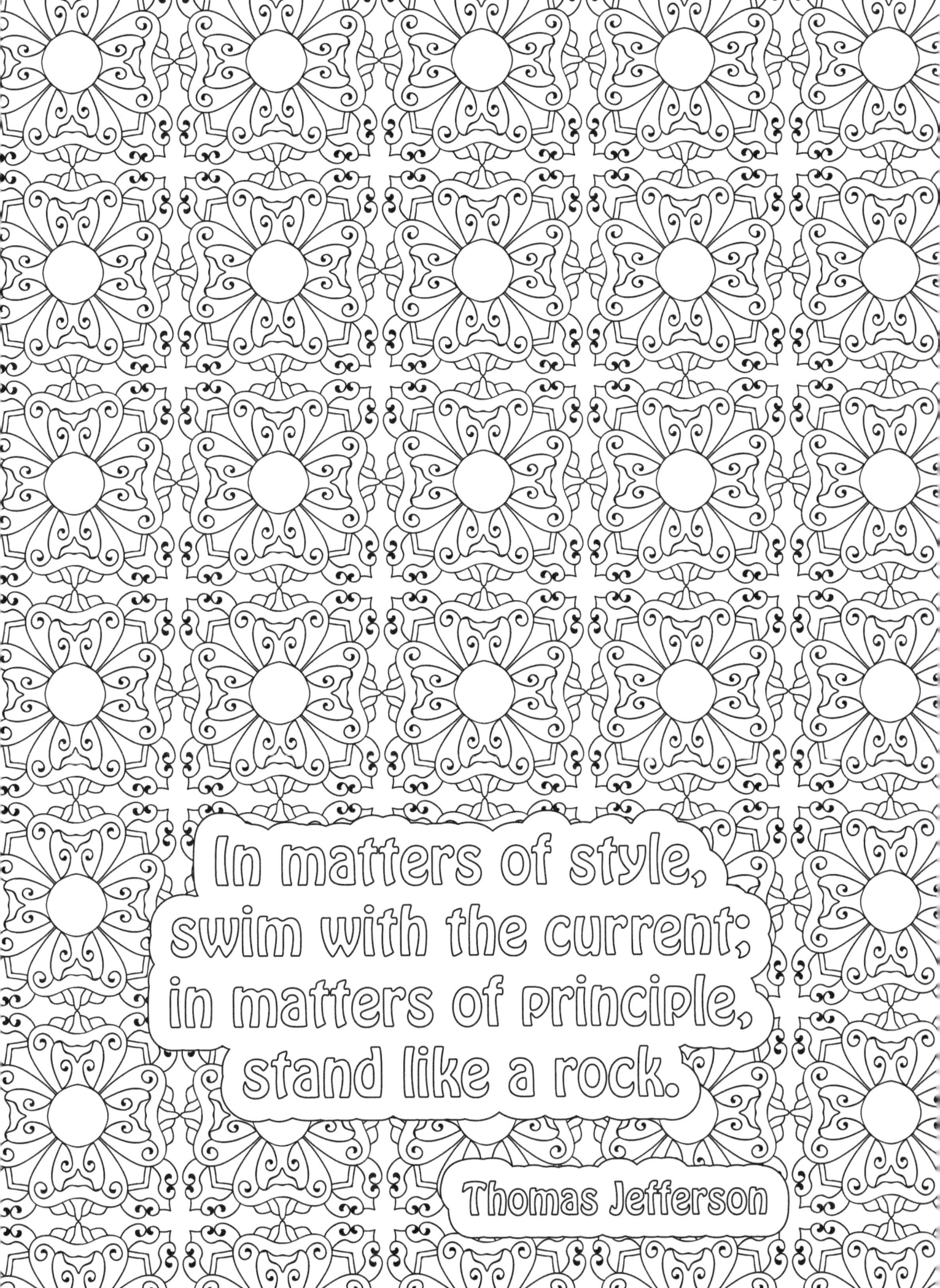

In matters of style, swim with the current; in matters of principle, stand like a rock.

Thomas Jefferson

For more designs and upcoming books, please visit our facebook group at :

@coloringbooksandmandalas

http://www.asmazergui.com